SAVI

A FAITH-FILLED GUIDE TO OWNING YOUR PERSONALITY, YOUR PAST & YOUR PURPOSE

BRITTANY WHITE

Copyright © 2025 by Brittany White

All rights reserved. This book or any portion thereof may not be reproduced or used in any manner whatsoever without the expressed written permission of the author except for the use of brief quotations in a book review.

ISBN: 979-8-9987448-0-8 (Paperback)
      979-8-9987448-1-5 (eBook)

Printed in the United States of America.

First printing, 2025.

Brittany White
1208 N. Main Street
Suite G
Suffolk, VA. 23434
www.savedgirlsummer.com
Email: info@savedgirlsummer.com

DEDICATION

This manual is dedicated to the women who have ever felt like they didn't belong—the ones who sat in church but felt unseen, who loved God but questioned if He had space for them as they were.

To the misfits, the outcasts, the in-betweeners, and the ones who never quite fit the mold—this is for you. You are not too much. You are not alone. You are exactly who God intended you to be.

May these pages remind you that you are loved, chosen, and purposed. You belong in His kingdom, and you belong here.

With love,

Brittany

TABLE OF CONTENTS

Preface xii

Introduction xix

Chapter One .... 01 - 06

Chapter Two .... 07 - 12

Chapter Three .... 13 - 18

Chapter Four .... 19 - 29

Chapter Five .... 31 - 40

Chapter Six .... 41 - 47

Chapter Seven .... 49 - 56

Chapter Eight .... 57 - 58

Acknowledgments 61

Author Photo 62

About the Author 63

Connect with the Author 64

PREFACE

From Misfit to Ministry: Why I Wrote This Book

I didn't always feel like I belonged in church. Growing up as a preacher's kid—times two, mind you—I was immersed in faith, but I never quite saw anyone like me reflected in ministry. I didn't see women who looked, talked, or acted like me in leadership, and I often felt like the rules of the church were holding me back from the freedom I craved.

As a teenager, I dreamed of growing up and experiencing the world in all its fullness—what I thought was "fun." That absence of representation caused me to search for acceptance in places and with people outside of the church.

It is from that place of rediscovering my worth and purpose in Him that Saved Girl Summer was born. What started as a small desire to connect with women like me—women who didn't fit the conventional mold of faith—has turned into a movement. A movement that celebrates the beauty, power, and authenticity of women who are often overlooked or misunderstood in the church.

This book is my story, my journey, and a guide for women who might feel like they don't belong. Let my testimony—and the stories of the biblical women you'll meet in these pages—remind you that your past doesn't disqualify you from living out your purpose.

I'm not perfect, and I haven't always had it all figured out. In fact, for a long time, I thought my background and struggles made me unworthy. But now, I see that those very things—my story, my flaws, my unique identity—are exactly what God has used to create something meaningful.

I'll never forget the moment—tear-filled and trembling—when I gave God my "YES." That didn't mean accepting His plan was easy. When He called me to say yes to His will, I wrestled with doubt.

How could God use someone like me—someone with a past, someone who didn't fit the typical mold of a ministry leader?

That's when God began to speak to me about creating a ministry that would help bring healing to broken women. Still wrestling with self-doubt, I asked Him,

> *"God, how can You use me to help heal others when I'm so broken myself?"*

But in those moments of hesitation, He whispered Isaiah 61:3: His promise **"to give beauty for ashes."** God was reminding me that He would take every part of my past and use it to create something beautiful.

I've learned that the church, faith, and ministry don't follow a one-size-fits-all model. God is still in the business of using all kinds of women, with all kinds of stories, to do His work.

So, if you've ever felt like you didn't fit in, or like you had too many flaws to be used by God, this book is for you. I wrote it because I know what it feels like to be that woman who feels out of place. But more importantly, I wrote it because I know what it feels like to be called by God and to finally understand that He's been preparing you all along for something extraordinary.

> *"'You are fearfully and wonderfully made.'*
> *You are exactly who God created you to be—*
> *and He can use every part of you."*

INTRODUCTION

Hey Girl! Welcome to Saved Girl Season

Hey Girl! Hey! Welcome to the ultimate guide for Saved Girls! This isn't just another book—it's your guide to navigating faith, fun, and freedom as a young woman of God.

If you've ever felt like living for Christ meant giving up excitement, style, or your social life, think again. This book is here to help you embrace a faith-filled life without sacrificing your personality, your passion, or your purpose.

By the time you turn the last page, my prayer is that you will see yourself the way God sees you—not as someone waiting to be accepted, but as a woman who already belongs in God's plan.

Let me introduce myself—I'm Brittany White, founder of *Saved Girl Summer*. But more than that, I'm a woman who's been where you are. That's why I started *Saved Girl Summer* in 2021: to build a community for women who feel like they don't fit the traditional church mold.

We're the ones who may have been overlooked or told we didn't belong. We're the women who have made mistakes but know that God is still able to use us. This movement is for us—to embrace who we are in Christ and walk confidently in our purpose, no matter our past.

Saved Girl is all about confidence, community, and Christ-centered living. Whether you're working on your relationship with God, strengthening your friendships, or figuring out how to balance faith with everyday life, this book is packed with wisdom, encouragement, and practical steps to help you thrive.

Inside, you'll find real talk about relationships, purpose, self-care, and navigating today's culture as a faith-filled woman. No more feeling like an outsider—this is your season to shine, to grow, and to walk boldly in who God created you to be.

So grab your Bible, your journal, and maybe a cute highlighter or two—because ***Saved Girl* season starts now!**

CHAPTER ONE
FROM REBELLION TO REDEMPTION

How God Can Use Our History to Protect Our Future

Embracing God's Plan for Me

Teenage me had it all figured out... or so I thought. I was going to have all the fun my lil' happy hips could handle until I turned 40. Why 40, you ask? Because we all know that when you're a teenager, turning 40 means you've officially become a senior citizen. I was going to celebrate my 40th with a bang and then have a "come to Jesus" moment. I'd give my life back to the Lord, cut out all my foolishness, and go on The 700 Club to give my testimony of how I went from running the streets to running for Jesus!

I would often share this plan with my mother, who would always remind me, "That's not who you are." Being 16 and thinking I knew everything, I couldn't fathom how my own mother—the woman who birthed me and raised me—thought she knew the plans for my life better than I did. What I didn't consider was that my mom was a praying woman with a real relationship with Jesus.

While I thought my plan to live life and be the "Black Britney Spears" (I've always been an entertainer at heart—and Brit was THAT GIRL in my high school days) was divinely influenced, my mama knew that wasn't what God had planned for me.

When Life Starts Life'n

Now, if I'm being totally honest, for a few years I did have fun. I'm talking about Vanessa Huxtable having big fun with the wretched in Baltimore type of fun. But then life started "life'n," and I found myself running back to the same God I had tried so hard to run from.

Just like the father of the prodigal son, He was right there to celebrate my return. It was during this time that God first started giving me glimpses of what He had in store for me. So I had a decision to make: would I be disobedient, or would I give Him my yes?

One of the main reasons I hesitated was because I thought I had done too much and messed up too badly for God to use me. Another reason? I didn't see many women in ministry who looked like me or lived like me. I honestly thought God might have confused my assignment with someone else's.

I felt the need to remind the Lord that I liked *Mary Mary* AND *Mary J. Blige*. I preferred stilettos over kitten heels, and lace closure wigs over lace chapel caps. Could God really use someone like me? That's when He reminded me of Psalm 139:13–14 (KJV):

> *"For thou hast possessed my reins:*
> *thou hast covered me in my mother's womb.*
> *I will praise thee; for I am fearfully and wonderfully made:*
> *marvelous are thy works;*
> *and that my soul knoweth right well."*

God was reassuring me that He knew exactly who I was because He created me that way—and that He was going to use the very things I thought disqualified me for His glory.

RAHAB'S REDEMPTION
How Her Past Became Part of God's Plan

I love how the Bible is full of people who others would label as "disqualified." A perfect example? RAHAB.

In the Bible, Rahab is referred to as a harlot—a woman who sold her body for money. To borrow a line from the cinematic classic The Players Club, before there was Ronnie, Rahab was in Jericho "using what she got to get what she want."

Like most fallen women in Scripture, we don't get much of Rahab's backstory. We don't know what choices she made to end up in the world's oldest profession. But I like to believe that Rahab, for reasons unknown to us, was in a position where she had to care for her family.

In a society where women were usually provided for by men, it's possible Rahab had to take on the role of provider. And let's be real—employment options for women back then were slim to none. So even though she was technically a "working girl," when it was all said and done, Rahab was just a girl working to survive.

Courage in a Crisis

When we meet Rahab in Joshua chapter 2, the Israelites have sent spies into the land to scope out Jericho:

> *"Now therefore, I pray you, swear unto me by the LORD,*
> *since I have shewed you kindness,*
> *that ye will also shew kindness unto my father's house,*
> *and give me a true token:*
> *And that ye will save alive my father,*
> *and my mother, and my brethren, and my sisters,*
> *and all that they have, and deliver our lives from death.*
> *And the men answered her, Our life for yours,*
> *if ye utter not this our business..."*
> **~ Joshua 2:12–14 KJV ~**

When the king of Jericho heard the spies were in town, he reached out to Rahab. He figured if anyone knew where the men were, it would be her.

Once the king's men were gone, Rahab helped the spies escape—after making them promise to protect her family. And they did. When the Israelites returned and conquered Jericho, Rahab and her household were spared.

ROMANS 8:28 IN ACTION:
From Mistakes to Miracles— How God Transforms Your Past for His Purpose

I find it wild that Rahab's profession was the very thing God used to save her family. Her job gave the spies a cover story. No one questioned two men going into her house. It made sense based on her reputation.

But isn't that just like God?

Romans 8:28 reminds us that *"all things work together for good to them that love God."* ALL things. Not just the clean and cute things. Not just the "church-approved" parts. God can use the very things we're ashamed of—the things that made us feel unworthy—for His glory.

Rahab's story shows us that your past isn't powerful enough to cancel your future. The same woman whose name once brought shame became part of Jesus' lineage.

Let that sink in.

SAVED GIRL SESSION
Your Turn to Reflect, Heal, and Share

Like Rahab, we all have a history. When you think about your past, are you proud of your progress—or still stuck in self-condemnation?

Remember:
> *"There is therefore now no condemnation to them which are in Christ Jesus."*
> **~ Romans 8:1 KJV ~**

Rahab didn't let her past stop her from securing a future for herself and generations after her. And neither should you.

Take time to reflect:

- How far have you come?
- Are you willing to share your story to help someone else?

Pray about it.
Then start writing.

Use the space provided to begin crafting your testimony and noting life lessons God has taught you. Someone out there needs to hear what He's brought you through. Your past might just be the key to unlocking someone else's healing.

_____
_____
_____
_____
_____

CHAPTER TWO
ELIGIBILITY REQUIREMENTS
WHY JESUS CALLS YOU SAVED

From Hot Girl to His Girl

Calling all former hot girls and retired city girls! Whether you are an "OG" Saved Girl or just starting your relationship with God, all sisters are eligible to join in "Saved Girl Season." PERIOD! The only requirement is that you commit to your process of evolving into your best self and pushing and supporting your sisters along the way.

Are You a Saved Girl?

Saved Girls come from all walks of life. They are of every race, age, and color. They come from various financial and educational backgrounds. Differences aside, they all share two things in common: their love for Jesus and their desire to let Him use them! If that sounds like you, then guess what? You're a Saved Girl!

Now That You're In . . . What's Next?

Well, sis, that depends on you! What is God calling you to do? As Saved Girls, we realize that "ministry" comes in many different forms. That means that what God has called you to do may take place outside of the traditional four walls of the church. Ministry for you may look like speaking words of affirmation into your clients as you style their hair. Or maybe encouraging your coworkers when you see them having a bad day.

The main thing is that you ask God what His plan is for your life and partner with Him on it. What He's calling you to do may not look like what He's called other people to do, and that's okay! As long as you're following His lead, then you can walk in confidence knowing that you are walking in your purpose.

There's an old saying that goes, "You may be the only Bible that some people ever read," meaning you should live your life in a way that draws people to Jesus even if they've never read the Bible or been to church. Now let me put this in Saved Girl terms: Sis, you may be the only "Saved Girl Guide" that another woman ever reads, so live your life in a way that makes them want to see what this "Saved Girl Life" is all about!

THE WOMAN WITH THE ALABASTER BOX
Breaking Boxes

In a house full of people more qualified than her, more "religious" than her and with more status than her, the woman with the alabaster box was the only one willing to minister to Jesus in a very personal way. Through the act of washing Jesus' feet with her tears and drying them with her hair, she set herself apart from the religious figures that surrounded her.

So how did a woman like herself find her way into the company of Jesus? Well, Jesus had been invited to the home of a Pharisee. Pharisees were a small but influential group of Jews who emphasized observance of the law and their own traditions as the path to righteousness. They looked down on people they considered less "holy." With her checkered past, the woman with the alabaster box fit into that "less than holy" category.

When she showed up uninvited to the Pharisee's house and began to anoint Jesus' feet with her oil and tears and dry them with her hair, the religious folk in the room were appalled. They even began to question Jesus, because surely if He was a prophet like He claimed, He wouldn't allow this woman to talk to Him, let alone touch Him! But in true Jesus fashion, He got them all the way together!

This woman proved that ministry doesn't always look like what we are used to, nor is it always done by the people that we would expect. She also proves that some eligibility rules, much like alabaster boxes, are meant to be broken.

Scripture Reference:

> *"Wherefore I say unto thee, her sins, which are many, are forgiven; for she loved much: but to whom little is forgiven, the same loveth little. And he said unto her, Thy sins are forgiven."*
> **~ Luke 7:40-48 KJV ~**

The Power of Her Pour

The woman with the alabaster box lived a sinful life. Like most of the other "sinful" women in the Bible, we are not told her exact sin, but it's safe to assume that whatever it was, it had caused her to be ostracized. So, a woman of her reputation showing up uninvited to a Pharisee's home proved just how desperate she was for an encounter with Jesus.

She braved the stares and the whispers because the healing that she needed was more important than what others thought about her. She took her jar of alabaster and poured the oil on His feet. A jar full of that oil was worth almost a year's wages for most people during that time—that's how valuable a moment with Jesus was to her.

She then washed His feet with her tears and dried them with her hair. This is significant because in that time, travel was mostly done on dusty roads. When visiting someone's home, water would be provided to wash your feet—usually a job for the lowest servants. And yet this woman did this unprompted, using her most precious possessions. She used the expensive oil to anoint Him and her hair—her crown—to dry His feet.

I believe that at that moment, there was a transfer that took place between her and Jesus. She cleaned His feet, and in turn, He cleaned her life. Although the Pharisee invited Jesus into his home, he did not do a good job of making Him feel welcome. Maybe it was his own self-righteous attitude. Yet we have this woman, whose sins are many, showering Jesus with affection.

Can you relate to the woman with the Alabaster Box? I know I can! When I stop to think about all the mistakes I've made and how Jesus still loves me, I can't help but get emotional. While we may not have expensive oil, Jesus is still welcoming us to pour out our hearts. He still welcomes our tears, whether of gratitude or grief. Like the Woman with the Alabaster Box, He invites us to lay our "crowns" at His feet.

SAVED GIRL SESSION
Your Turn to Reflect, Heal, and Share

Think about the Woman with the Alabaster Box and the courage it must've taken to approach Jesus in a room full of her harshest critics. Yet she pressed her way in because she knew one encounter with Jesus was worth it.

Now think about what is in your "alabaster box." Imagine yourself in a room with Jesus. What do you need to pour at His feet? Are they your worries? Your painful memories? Maybe you just need a moment to pour out your praise. Whatever it is, take some time and pour it out.

Then once you are finished pouring, leave it there. Just like the oil couldn't be placed back in the alabaster box, Jesus forgave this woman's sins so that they were no longer a part of who she was. Allow Him to do the same with your pour.

_____
_____
_____
_____
_____
_____
_____
_____
_____
_____
_____
_____

CHAPTER THREE

COMMUNITY AND CONNECTION
Faith Together

To paraphrase Sister Cyndi Lauper: *"Saved Girls Just Want to Have Fun."* That's literally in our *Saved Girl* motto—**"Where Faith, Fabulous, and FUN Meet."** But I didn't always believe it was possible to love God and enjoy life.

When I first got serious about my relationship with God, I mourned what I thought I was leaving behind—fun. In my mind, being "Saved" meant being serious all the time. Thank God He showed me otherwise. A real relationship with Him is the opposite of boring.

The problem was that I didn't see many opportunities to hang out with other women of faith outside of traditional church settings. So I created some! Events where women could come together to have fun and fellowship—but also walk away filled with the Word.

Here's a glimpse at some of the events we've hosted:

Saved Girl Summer Brunch

Our flagship event. The *Saved Girl Summer Brunch* brings Saved Girls together for a lil' brunch and a whole lotta Bible! Each brunch is centered around a fun theme and a biblical woman.

One of our past themes was *"Saved Girls Taking Over for the '99 and the 2000s."* Picture this: a DJ, karaoke, décor inspired by late-90s and early-2000s fashion, and women creating a "mixtape" based on their life's greatest hits. I mean... where else can you dance battle before Bible study?

Saved Girl Summer Paint Night

If you're an 80s or 90s baby, chances are you remember Bob Ross. I don't know if the anointing was in his paintbrush or his 'fro, but the man could start with splatters and end up with a masterpiece.

Inspired by his philosophy of "happy little accidents," our *Saved Girl Summer Paint Night* centers on the idea that God—the Master Artist—can take our mess and turn it into a masterpiece. Women leave with more than just a painting. They leave reminded that they are *one of God's greatest masterpieces*.

> "Jesus loves you enough to meet you where you are, but too much to let you stay there."

Fun is part of our events, but our main goal is for women to have a real encounter with Jesus. He's the One who meets us right in the middle of our mess. He doesn't wait until we've got it all together.

Some of us, like the prodigal son, have to be met in the "pig pens" of life before we realize how much we need Him. Still, He's always there—ready to welcome us home.

THE SAMARITAN WOMAN
How One Meetup With Jesus Can Change Your Life

Let me introduce you to one of my favorite women in the Bible. I like to call her the Samaritan City Girl. Now, she didn't get "flewed out"—she probably got cameled out by several different men around town. She was out in those Samaritan streets, and her reputation made her a social outcast. That's why she went to draw water in the hottest part of the day. Everyone else came early or late, when it was cooler. But not her—she wanted to avoid the stares and whispers.

All they saw was a five-time divorcée living with man number six. But they didn't know her story. They didn't know her why.

Maybe she had low self-esteem. Maybe she didn't know her worth. Maybe she was just looking for someone—anyone—to love her back. But then... she met Jesus.

Can't We All Just Get Along?
(A Quick History Lesson on the Jews and Samaritans Beef)

Samaritans were mixed—part Jewish, part something else. Because of that, the Jewish people looked down on them and avoided their region completely. So imagine the Samaritan woman's surprise when she sees Jesus, a Jewish man, sitting at her well and asking her for a drink.

Shocked, she asks, "Why are you talking to me?"

Jesus tells her He has "living water"—and that whoever drinks it will never thirst again.

Now sis was "thirsty" in every sense of the word, so of course she wants some of that water!

This is where Jesus gets her attention in a very Jesus-like way. He tells her to go get her husband.

Sis replies, "I have no husband."

Jesus is like, *"Correct—you've had five, and the one you're with now? Not yours either."*

Oops! Talk about heavenly shade. But here's the thing—when Jesus reads you, He doesn't read you for filth. He reads you up out of your filth. He sees you, knows you, loves you—and still calls you.

From their brief conversation, Tthe Samaritan Woman realizes Jesus must be a prophet. But He lets her know He's not just a prophet. He is the Messiah.

She's so amazed, she runs back into the city to tell everyone, *"Come, see a man who told me everything I've ever done!"*

The Bible says:
> *"And many of the Samaritans of that city*
> *believed on him for the saying of the woman...*
> *And many more believed because of His own word...*
> *Now we believe, not because of thy saying:*
> *for we have heard Him ourselves,*
> *and know that this is indeed the Christ, t*
> *he Savior of the world."*
> **~ John 4:39–42 (KJV) ~**

Sis literally went from hot mess to holy messenger.

That's the power of one encounter with Jesus. Think about it. He didn't have to stop at that well. He definitely didn't have to say anything to her. Yet, He chose to go out of His way to meet with her. And guess what? He'll do the same thing for you.

So, sis...

WHERE'S YOUR WELL?

Where do you need Jesus to meet you?
What area of your life feels dry, overused, or empty?

Sit down for a moment and talk to Jesus.

SAVED GIRL SESSION
Let's Take a Moment to Reflect

Consider what areas in your life are a "well"? These are the places where you feel stuck, thirsty, or not put together.

Make a list below, then match each "well" with a "living water" scripture.

Example:

My Well: Anxiety

The Living Water: Philippians 4:6-7 — "Do not be anxious about anything, but in every situation, by prayer and petition, with thanksgiving, present your requests to God. And the peace of God, which transcends all understanding, will guard your hearts and your minds in Christ Jesus."

No matter what your well may be, God has already made provision—through His Son and through His Word—to meet you there.

_____
_____
_____
_____
_____
_____
_____
_____
_____
_____

CHAPTER FOUR
SAVED GIRL DATING

Navigating Love, Boundaries, and Godly Relationships

As a *Saved Girl*, there are certain standards we carry when it comes to dating and relationships. Sis, I know you want a relationship—but don't let loneliness or desperation put you in something you'll have to pray your way out of later. You are the daughter of the King, and last I checked, the princess doesn't fall for the court jester and live happily ever after!

Yet, here we are... falling for court jesters and wondering why it never works out.

The Bible tells us not to cast our pearls before swine (Matthew 7:6). In other words, don't give valuable things to people who won't appreciate them. And I can't think of anything more valuable than your body, your mind, and your heart. So why hand those over to someone who doesn't even know what to do with them?

Now, I'd be lying if I said I didn't have to learn this the hard way. I've given my heart to a pig or two myself. It's because of those lessons that I can confidently encourage you to wait on the man that God has for you.

Let's Talk About SEX

I already know some of the Saints are clutching their pearls at the mention of the word—but it's time the church stops pretending sex doesn't exist and starts getting real about it. Because... if none of the Saints are having sex, then where are all these little Saints coming from?

Let's be honest—clearly the altar isn't the only place where folks are "laying hands." But instead of hiding the conversation in shame or silence, we need to talk about sex in a healthy, godly, and honest way.

Now PLEASE don't take this as a green light to get down with whomever, whenever. Yes, sex is a beautiful thing—but God designed it to be shared between a **husband and wife**. Not your boyfriend, not your boo thang, not your sneaky link… your **HUZZZBAND**.

And if you're saying, "Girrrrllll, that ship has sailed for me. I can't get my virginity back, so what now?"

I'm glad you asked.

I Was That Girl, Too

I remember sitting at what felt like my 50-11th youth conference as a teenager. The topic was celibacy (again), and the speaker just so happened to be the Pastor's niece. She stood proudly on stage sharing how she was 27 years old and still a virgin.

Now… I was 17 at the time and already had more experience than I care to admit. All I heard was "27-year-old virgin" and I tuned the rest out. I remember thinking, "Well dang… what's the point of waiting now?" And that's the problem. So many of us are told **not** to have sex—but we're never told **why**.

The Messages That Shaped Me

As a church girl, I was told, "Don't have sex before marriage—it's a sin." Dassit. No breakdown. No deeper explanation.

Meanwhile, female rappers like Lil' Kim and Trina were preaching the power of sexuality. These women walked so the Megs and Cardis of the world could run. And as a young girl? I ate it up. They had style. They had confidence. They didn't "need" a man. They were in control.

So after a couple heartbreaks in high school, I told myself I'd be a player too. If guys could do it, why couldn't I? Except... I was terrible at that life.

If Trina was the "Diamond Princess," I was the **Cubic Zirconia Queen**.

I wasn't getting spoiled. I wasn't being taken on trips. I was buying them stuff—PlayStations, Jordan's, jerseys. I was giving away my body and my money. And all I had to show for it? Empty pockets... and an even emptier soul.

What the Church (and Rap Songs) Didn't Teach Me

No one taught us about **soul ties**.

> *"And they twain shall be one flesh:*
> *so then they are no more twain,*
> *but one flesh."*
> **~ Mark 10:8 KJV ~**

Sex isn't just physical. It's spiritual. It's emotional. It's soul-deep. And when you become "one flesh" with someone—your soul attaches to theirs. That's why it was so hard for me to walk away from the situationships I knew weren't good for me. Yeah, situationships—those "we're more than friends but not really a couple" setups where someone always ends up catching feelings.

Spoiler alert: IT WAS ALWAYS ME!

I'd find myself trying to prove I was girlfriend material—cooking, cleaning, sexing—hoping they'd see me as "wifey." But listen closely:

> **"IF YOU HAVE TO PROVE YOUR WORTH TO A MAN,**
> **HE'S NOT YOUR MAN."**

I know reading and processing that may be tough, but it is the truth. As hard as it may be to realize, understand that no amount of doing or buying will make a man stay if he doesn't want to.

He's Just Not That Into You

I'll never forget watching an interview with the author of *He's Just Not That Into You*. I don't remember a word he said—but that title hit me like a ton of bricks. Because deep down, I knew. The guy I was dealing with? He wasn't into me. He was into my body. And even though he said from the jump that he didn't want a relationship—I thought I could change his mind.

> "If he didn't care, why would he have me over? Why would he spend time with me? He must care more about me than he wants to admit, right?"

WRONG.

He wasn't invested in me—he was invested in what I could give him. But because of the soul tie, I couldn't walk away. He wasn't my Prince Charming. And let's be real—I kissed a lot of frogs that never turned into anything.

Disney Dreams & Tattoos I Regret

Speaking of Prince Charming, I was obsessed with Disney Princesses as a kid. So obsessed that the second I turned 18, I ran to get my first tattoo: the word "Princess."

And where was it, you ask? Let's just say it rhymed with cramp stamp.

Keep in mind that this was 2005 and nothing went better with a pair of low-rise Applebottom jeans and boots with the fur then a lower-back tattoo. I didn't think about the fact that twenty years later I would still be walking around at my big age with the word "Princess" written in cursive on my back, but at eighteen it seemed like a logical thing to do.

From BUMAZ to Boaz

While Disney Princesses dreamed of the day they would be rescued by the handsome prince, little church girls like myself dreamed of the day that we would be rescued by our "Boaz." For us, Boaz was the Biblical equivalent of "Prince Charming." We were taught to wait for the man that God had for us, our Boaz. But sis ... let's be real. A lot of us, myself included, have dated one of his distant cousins instead.

When I was in college, his name was **BumAz**.

Now before you judge me—think about it. Don't act like you don't know that family tree. Maybe you're familiar with the brothers—**BrokeAz**, **CheatingAz**, or **LazyAz**.

What I didn't realize then is that Boaz wasn't just some handsome, rich man who came and scooped Ruth up like a fairytale. The real story is so much deeper than that. And once I learned the full picture, I realized that Ruth's story is not just about waiting—it's about ***preparation***, ***obedience***, and ***trusting*** God even in grief.

RUTH

"My Man, My Man, My Man."

Ruth Didn't Just Wait—She Prepared

When we meet Ruth in the Bible, she's not in a fairytale—she's in a **funeral**. Her husband is dead. Her brother-in-law is dead, and so is her father-in-law. And the only family she has left is her mother-in-law Naomi and her sister-in-law, Orpah.

Naomi is devastated, grieving, and ready to head back to her hometown in Bethlehem. She tells Ruth and Orpah to stay behind and go back to their own people. Orpah does just that, but Ruth? Ruth chooses to stay.

Ruth's response to Naomi was:

> *"Where you go, I will go.*
> *Where you stay, I will stay.*
> *Your people will be my people, and your God will be my God."*
> **~ Ruth 1:16 ~**
> *(paraphrased)*

Sis, Ruth made a choice—not just to stay with Naomi, but to walk into the unknown, trusting Naomi's God, trusting Naomi's wisdom, and trusting that her story wasn't over just because her heart was broken.

Obedience Opened the Door

When they get to Bethlehem, Ruth doesn't sit around waiting for a man to find her—she gets to work.

Back in those times, there were laws that allowed the poor and the widows to gather leftover grain in the fields. It was a form of provision—but it was also hard work and potentially dangerous for a woman alone. Ruth chooses to go out and glean in the fields to make sure she and Naomi can eat. And wouldn't you know it? The field she ends up in belongs to **Boaz**—a wealthy, respected landowner who also happens to be **a relative of Naomi's late husband**.

Boaz sees Ruth in the field and says to his workers, "Who is that?" But not in a creepy way—in a curious way.

Once he learns who she is and what she's done for Naomi, Boaz is impressed—not with her looks, but with her character. He tells his men not to touch her, and to even make sure she has extra grain. He tells Ruth to stay in his field, where she'll be safe and provided for. As you can imagine, Ruth is shook.

Ruth's responded to Boaz's favor by saying:

> "Why have I found favor in your eyes,
> that you should notice me—a foreigner?"
> ~ **Ruth 2:10** ~
> (paraphrased)

Because here's the thing—Ruth wasn't trying to be noticed. She was just being faithful. Still, Boaz noticed her because her character and value were showing through how she carried herself.
Though she wasn't looking, God sent favor to find Ruth while she was working and walking in purpose.

Sis, what are you doing in your waiting season?

Wise Counsel Will Guide You

Now, this is the part most people don't talk about. Ruth didn't throw herself at Boaz. She wasn't out here plotting in her DMs. She had wise counsel. Naomi, being seasoned and strategic, tells Ruth exactly what to do. She says:

> "Wash, put on your best clothes, anoint yourself with oil,
> and go down to the threshing floor...
> then wait until Boaz has finished eating and drinking...
> lie at his feet and he will tell you what to do."
> ~ **Ruth 3:3-4** ~
> (paraphrased)

And what does Ruth do?

> "All that you say, I will do."
> ~ **Ruth 3:5** ~

Sis, Ruth wasn't out here asking for advice from her homegirl who still answers her ex's texts. She listened to someone who had wisdom, fruit, and godly perspective. Ruth humbled herself, trusted Naomi, and followed the instructions.

Wise Counsel vs Wrong Advice?

"HE'S A GOOD MAN, SAVANNAH."

Y'all remember that scene from *Waiting to Exhale*, right? Whitney Houston's character was being told by her mother to keep seeing a man... even though he was married.

I remember watching that thinking, "Girl, Whet?!"

But that's exactly what happens when we lean on familiar voices instead of faithful voices. It's easy to turn to our close friends and family for advice—but are they really qualified for the job? I know she's your favorite cousin, but after three divorces and two baby daddies, is she really the person you want giving you relationship advice?

Now don't get me wrong—I'm not shaming anybody. Life is hard and relationships don't always work out. But let me ask you this:

Would you go to your beautician for an oil change?

Unless she runs a beauty salon AND an auto body shop—(and if she does, shout out to our multiple-streams-of-income queens)—that's not the right person for that job. Same goes for love and relationships.

People may mean well, but before you follow their advice, you've got to check their fruit.

"Ye shall know them by their fruits.
Do men gather grapes of thorns, or figs of thistles?
Even so every good tree bringeth forth good fruit;
but a corrupt tree bringeth forth evil fruit."
~ **Matthew 7:16-17 KJV** ~

Ruth Knew Who to Listen To

Ruth didn't just listen to Naomi because she liked her—she listened because Naomi's life had fruit. Even in her grief, Naomi had wisdom. Ruth trusted her counsel enough to leave her homeland, follow her into the unknown, and eventually obey her advice about how to approach Boaz. That's how serious godly counsel is.

Redemption Is Possible

Now here's where it gets even better. Boaz wasn't just any man—he was what they called a **kinsman redeeme**r—restoring her family, her finances, and her heart. That meant he had the legal and spiritual ability to redeem the property, the family name, and even the future of Ruth and Naomi. He didn't just offer protection—he offered **restoration**. Boaz made sure everything was done decently and in order. He met with the elders, confirmed he was eligible to redeem Ruth, and then... he MARRIED her. And sis, that union? It wasn't just a love story—it was legacy.

Ruth and Boaz gave birth to Obed, who became the father of Jesse... who became the father of David... and **through that lineage came JESUS**—the ultimate Redeemer.

He redeems reputations. He redeems broken hearts. He redeems the years you thought were wasted on the wrong one. So if you're carrying shame from your past, heartbreak from your present, or fear about your future—give it all to God. He can turn your ashes into beauty.

Real Talk

Ruth didn't chase Boaz. She followed God. And in doing so, she found healing, purpose, and love. She didn't let her past pain keep her from her future promise. And just in case you forgot—Boaz's mother was Rahab, the former harlot who hid the Israelite spies that we talked about in the previous chapter.

Yep! That's right! God took a woman with a scandalous past, and a woman with a broken heart, and used both of them to bring forth the Savior of the world. Now tell me God isn't a **REDEEMER**.

He has the power to take us from grief to **GLORY**, from heartbreak to **HEALING**, and from loss to **LEGACY**.

SAVED GIRL SESSION

When it comes to relationships, what season are you in right now?

Are you single, dating, married, divorced, or widowed?

No matter your status, you have purpose in this season.

Like Ruth, seek wise, godly counsel—and ask God to reveal your "Naomis." Those women who can trust to give you guidance and wisdom.

Or maybe... just maybe, God is calling you to be a Naomi to someone else.

Saved Girl Reflection:

Use the space below to write about your current relationship season. Ask God to show you one woman who may need your voice, your story, or your wisdom right now.

_____
_____
_____
_____
_____
_____
_____
_____
_____
_____
_____
_____
_____
_____

CHAPTER FIVE

SEEN, HEARD & LOVED

The God Who Sees You
(Even When You Don't See Yourself)

Somewhere between Proverbs 31 and 90s R&B...

there's me.

There are a few people who, in the eyes of the African American community, can do no wrong. Jesus, followed by Martin Luther King, Jr., automatically come to mind. If I had my way, there are three more names that would be added to that list: Kirk Franklin and Tina and Erica Campbell of "Mary Mary."

Now hear me out. I know Jesus and MLK are hard acts to follow, but Kirk Franklin and Mary Mary will always hold a special place in my lil' church kid heart. Why? Because they made church music cool. I know some would argue that they weren't the first to make mainstream crossover hits in Gospel music, but you can't deny the fact that they brought Gospel music to the masses on a whole new level.

Picture it, Sicily 1923. (If you're a Golden Girls fan, you'll get that reference.) Okay, picture it for real this time: Dinwiddie County, VA, 1997. A young girl is riding a school bus when her best friend asks her, "Have you heard that new Kirk Franklin song, 'Stomp?'" That young girl was me, and that song would be one that helped change how I viewed myself as a "Church Kid."

For the first time in my life, there was a song I could sing along to with my unchurched friends. Now if "Stomp" made the Saints clutch their pearls, then Mary Mary's "Shackles" came to finish the job by snatching them up by their good church wigs.

While some of the older Saints were in a tizzy, younger Saints like myself were happy to finally have music we could not only move to but that also had a message.

I remember seeing Mary Mary in their music videos and thinking, "Wow, they look like me!" They had micro braids and cute outfits, and their videos were being played on Video Gospel and 106 & Park. I felt seen. And to a little girl who felt invisible and out of place in the world she grew up in, that was life-changing.

HAGAR & EL ROI AND THE GOD WHO SEES:
From "Melodies From Heaven" to the Middle of the Wilderness

Have you ever been out and heard someone say, "I see you!"? That usually means the person receiving the compliment is either looking really fly or has done something that has caused the other person to recognize them. Those three little words can have a major impact.

Hagar knew how it felt to finally be seen. In a world where she was often overlooked, she had a personal encounter with El Roi—the God who sees me.

I'm a firm believer that if somebody tells you the Bible is boring, they haven't actually read it. The Bible is filled with drama, and as a recovering ratchet reality TV addict (God is still working on me), I must admit that stories like Hagar's really interest me.

Hagar was an Egyptian slave who belonged to Abraham's wife, Sarah, and through no fault of her own, found herself in the middle of what I like to refer to as Biblical baby mama drama.

God had promised Abraham that He would make him the father of many nations; however, Sarah was unable to have children. At this point in their story, both Abraham and Sarah are very old.

Sarah, giving up on the possibility of giving her husband a biological child of her own, comes up with the brilliant idea of giving her servant Hagar to Abraham so that he can have a child with her. I think Sarah called herself trying to help God out. The problem with trying to help God out is this:

#1. **HE DOESN'T NEED OUR HELP!**

#2. We usually just end up making things worse instead of actually helping.

In essence, Hagar is given to Abraham as a second wife. If being a slave isn't bad enough, she is now being forced to marry this old man and have his child. Sarah did not see Hagar as someone worthy of being given the option to say yes or no to her plan. To her, Hagar was nothing more than a baby incubator.

Now this is where the drama starts. While Sarah had planned on Hagar getting pregnant, what she hadn't planned on was the way that Hagar would start feeling herself after she did.

"And he went in unto Hagar, and she conceived: and when she saw that she had conceived, her mistress was despised in her eyes."
~ *Genesis 16:4 KJV* ~

Baabbeee, Hagar got pregnant, and you couldn't tell her nothing!

As I'm sure you can imagine, this caused tension between Sarah and Abraham, with Sarah blaming him for Hagar's bad attitude. Wanting no parts of it, Abraham was like:

> "My name is Bennett and I ain't in it!"

And in pure dismissive fashion, Abraham told Sarah to do whatever she thought was best with Hagar.

It's My Fault but You're to Blame

As the Bible explains, Sarah begins to mistreat Hagar, so much so that Hagar runs away. Sarah's plan has backfired, and she finds herself still childless while Hagar finds herself alone and pregnant in the desert.

Now I want to pause for a second and say that although I don't condone Sarah's behavior, I can somewhat understand it. Sarah and Hagar lived during a time when barrenness in women was the cause of great shame and in some instances even considered a curse. Women were supposed to get married and give their husbands sons to continue the family legacy. How was her husband going to be the father of many nations when she couldn't even give him one child?

Pretty Hurts

Once we delve a little further into Sarah's story we learn that much like Hagar, she was used to being "unseen." Although she was physically beautiful, her beauty put her in situations where her husband Abraham, fearing for his safety, made her lie to protect him. Twice he made her lie to kings and pretend to be his sister. Wanting to protect her husband she followed his plans, even if that meant being taken into the household of another man.

> "Even people who we view as 'having it all together' because of their position or title—if they have unresolved hurt—can still hurt others."

You would think that these experiences of not having any say-so over her own body would have caused Sarah to act kinder towards Hagar, but it seemed to do the opposite.

Once given a position of power, Sarah did the same thing to Hagar that Abraham had done to her. Though Sarah was beautiful, she was barren--physically and emotionally. This I'm sure caused her to feel insecure and inadequate as a woman, and especially as a wife.

How many times have we encountered women like Sarah in our lives? Women who seemed to have it all on the outside, but still felt the need to tear down other women. Maybe it was a former boss who you could never seem to satisfy at work no matter how hard you tried. Or maybe it was the most popular girl in your high school who, although voted prom queen and most likely to succeed, still picked on the less popular girls.

Situations like these leave us wondering why women with success and popularity would still hurt other women. I know it sounds cliche, but it really is true that "hurt people hurt people." Oftentimes as women, when we are hurt or dealing with insecurities, we tend to project those things onto others. Sarah was insecure about her inability to give her husband a child. This caused her to not only force Hagar to be a part of her plan, but to then turn around and mistreat her because of it.

MINI SAVED GIRL SESSION

Have you ever been hurt by someone you looked up to spiritually? How did that experience affect your relationship with God, others, or even yourself? Write out what healing from that could look like for you.

___
___
___
___

When God Steps Into the Wilderness

*"And she called the name of the LORD that spake unto her,
Thou God seest me: for she said,
Have I also here looked after him that seeth me?"*
~ Genesis 16:13 KJV ~

Now back to Hagar. She is all alone in the desert when she has an encounter with an angel of the Lord. It is because of this encounter that she gives God the name "El Roi," which means "You are the God who sees me."

Here she was in the middle of the desert, alone, pregnant, and unwanted, but God sent her a reminder in this barren place that she wasn't forgotten and that He saw her.

Saved Girl, maybe you too have found yourself in a barren situation like Hagar, or maybe you are dealing with a form of barrenness on the inside like Sarah. Can I remind you that just like Hagar, God hasn't forgotten about you or lost sight of you or your promise? He sees you!!!

Just like Hagar found herself seen by God in the most barren of places, I too found myself seen through the melodies of Kirk Franklin and Mary Mary. There's something powerful about music—it can shift the atmosphere, minister to your spirit, and remind you of God's love. As you reflect on how God sees you, take a moment to immerse yourself in this Saved Girl Playlist. Let each song minister to your heart, reminding you that God is always present, always seeing, and always loving you.

SAVED GIRL SESSION

Think about a time in your life when you felt unseen. How did God show up to remind you that He was your El Roi?

Unlike people, God never loses sight of us, but sometimes, amid the hustle and bustle of life, we can lose sight of Him. Take some time to sit in His presence and allow Him to love on you.

Use this time alone with Him to let Him remind you that you are always seen by Him. Afterward, ask Him to show you ways that you can be someone's reminder of El Roi. It could be sending a quick text to your spouse to let them know that their hard work does not go unnoticed, or something as simple as paying someone you just met a compliment! What seems like a small gesture could be God using you to remind someone else that He sees them.

Use the lines below to plan out possible ways that you can be someone's reminder of "El Roi."

___
___
___
___
___
___
___
___
___
___
___
___
___
___
___
___
___

PRAISE, VIBES, AND HOLY HITS

Turn up the volume and let these songs be the soundtrack to your own Saved Girl Summer, or any other season for that matter!

Saved Girl, you've spent too long wondering if anyone truly sees the real you—the girl behind the glow up, the filter, the church shout. Just like Hagar out in that desert, feeling like no one cared about her story, you've questioned your value. But the same God who met her there is meeting you right here.

He's the God who sees you in your quiet moments and your loud ones. When you're feeling yourself and when you're falling apart. You don't have to prove yourself to Him. You don't have to perform. You're not an afterthought. You're an answer to someone's prayer, a solution to a problem, and God has placed something on the inside of you that's about to bless the world. You are seen, sis. Fully, completely, and without condition.

Whether you still have those anointed knees like our good sis Meg or had to retire them after Cash Money Records took over for the '99 and the 2000s, this playlist has something for all the Saved Girls.

SAVED GIRL PLAYLIST:

Pretty Girl Rock - Keri Hilson
You are fearfully and wonderfully made sis! You are cute and you know it, but more importantly, you know true beauty starts within. That's why you are working on getting healthy spiritually, emotionally, and physically. That healed pretty girl glow is another type of glow, and we love to see it!

God In Me - Mary Mary

Yeah, you cute or whateva, but let's not forget to give credit to the one who created you. When folks ask you how you manage to consistently serve God while serving looks, let them know it's the God in you!

Knuck If You Buck - Crime Mob

Because occasionally, you have to remind the Saints to pray with you, but DON'T play with you. Period.

Alabaster Box - CeCe Winans

After you finish all that knucking and bucking, you need a good ol' ugly cry song to get you back on track. What better than a song about redemption featuring a biblical baddie and her Alabaster Box?

Melodies From Heaven - Kirk Franklin and The Family

Because can you really call yourself a church kid if you don't know all the words to "Melodies from Heaven?" Before he was making us "Stomp" or asking if we wanted a "Revolution," Uncle Kirk had us all screaming "lelele-let it fall on meeeeee!"

CHAPTER SIX
SAVED GIRL DRESS CODE

Where Faith Meets Fashion

As a Saved Girl, I believe you can serve God while serving looks. Each of us is fearfully and wonderfully made, and we have every right to show that off. However, knowing who we are—and more importantly, WHOSE we are—means we don't have to show it all to make a statement! Sis, we know you're a "brick (church) house." When God was handing out booties, He definitely gave you "exceedingly and abundantly," but that doesn't mean you have to go around showing everything from your Genesis to your Revelation.

If I'm being honest, there was a time when I thought "less is more." The tighter or shorter the better! But as I grew older, I realized that I could still turn heads without showing e-ve-ry-thang.

> **Some divas are born, others are made.**
> I'd like to think I fell into the former category.

My mom often tells the story of how, when I was four years old, she found herself going toe-to-toe with a church mother on my behalf. As a baby fashionista, I decided I wanted to wear pink lip gloss to church one Sunday. This upset the aforementioned church mother, and she decided to set my mother straight. What she didn't know is that my mom—while very Holy—was also just a tad bit hood. She was knuckin' and buckin' and ready to fight in the natural AND the spirit. Trying to tell her how to raise her daughter was a no-no.

I think that event set the precedent for what would become not just my obvious love of fashion, but also my early feeling of being…**"TOO MUCH" for the church.** That feeling only intensified as I entered my teenage years.

Too Much for the Church? Or Just Enough for God?

It didn't take long for me to start questioning where I fit in—not just in the pew, but in the bigger picture of faith. The tension between wanting to express myself and feeling the pressure to tone it down left me wondering: Was I too bold? Too flashy? Too extra? But the more I learned about God, the more I began to understand—He didn't ask me to shrink. He created me with intention. And just enough for God doesn't mean less of me; it means the most of who He made me to be.

Now I'm about to keep it all the way real with y'all. In 1999, I turned 13. Many people remember it as the year the world became obsessed with Y2K. I remember it as the year Juvenile dropped his magnum opus, "Back That Thang Up," Sisqo devoted a whole song to undergarments, and Trina's booty was causing her to get pulled over. In other words, thick girls were getting celebrated, and as a lil' thickums, I was more than happy to not only shake but show off what my mama gave me.

As I entered high school, I noticed the attention my body got from boys—and I'd be lying if I said that attention didn't feel good. But teenage boys aren't the deepest individuals, and I found myself in several situations where I really liked a guy, but he was more interested in my body than my heart. That led me to believe, at a young age, that the most I had to offer a man was physical. I didn't realize that I was the daughter of a king, therfore I was royalty.

That being said, every woman has to make a personal decision on what she's comfortable wearing. Want to wear a crop top? Wear. The. Crop. Top. Sis! More comfortable in a turtleneck and kitten heels while serving "H.M.I.C.," Head Missionary in Charge realness? As Auntie Tab would say,

> *"That's your business."*

All I ask is that when in doubt about what to wear, consult with the Holy Spirit first. Like a loving Father, He's always there to offer gentle correction if and when we find ourselves taking it too far.

> *"Thou art all fair, my love; there is no spot in thee."*
> **~ Song of Solomon 4:7 KJV ~**

QUEEN ESTHER
A Lesson in How to Pray and Slay

The original "Queen B," Esther was the blueprint for serving God while serving looks. Her physical beauty got her into the kingdom, but her faith kept her there—and saved a nation.

Even though Esther was a queen, she wasn't born into royalty. In fact, her upbringing was anything but royal. Esther was an orphan raised by her cousin Mordecai. They lived in Persia under the rule of King Xerxes.

King Xerxes threw a party—not your average party either. This one lasted six months. Six months of straight partying! Even when I was out here "living my best life," I wouldn't have made it that long. Xerxes was in the palace partying like it was "1999" B.C. and decided he wanted to show off Queen Vashti. She was known for her beauty, and he couldn't wait to flex.

The only problem was—Vashti had her own party going on with her girls. When the king summoned her, she refused to come. That didn't sit well with King Xerxes or his boys. After consulting them, it was decided: Queen Vashti had to go.

Xerxes needed a new queen, so he sent for all the beautiful young virgins in his kingdom. Esther was among them. Mordecai warned her not to reveal her Jewish ancestry. Once inside the palace, Esther quickly found favor with the king's servant and eventually won the king's heart. The orphan girl had become queen.

But what she didn't realize was that God had placed her there for a reason.

Enter Haman—a full-time hater with a plan to destroy the Jews. When Mordecai found out, he urged Esther to speak up. But there was a problem: no one could go to the king uninvited. Doing so could mean death. Esther was afraid—understandably so.

Mordecai reminded her that silence wouldn't save her. If Haman's plan succeeded, she'd die too. He hit her with one of the most iconic lines in scripture:

> *"Then Mordecai commanded to answer Esther,*
> *Think not with thyself that thou shalt escape*
> *in the king's house, more than all the Jews.*
> *For if thou altogether holdest thy peace at this time,*
> *then shall there enlargement and deliverance*
> *arise to the Jews from another place;*
> *but thou and thy father's house shall be destroyed:*
> *and who knoweth whether thou art come to the kingdom*
> *for such a time as this?"*
> **~ Esther 4:13-14 KJV ~**

After Mordecai finished snatching her by her royal edges, Esther went into a time of fasting and prayer. From that place of faith, she created a plan. She found favor with the king—and saved her people.

Sis, you may not wear a crown (yet), but you were made royalty the moment you said yes to God. Like Esther, your purpose is bigger than your pain, past, or personality. Whether you're rocking a twist-out or a messy bun, a power suit or a hoodie, you were born for such a time as this.

Esther wasn't chosen just because she was fine (though sis was clearly slaying). She was chosen because God had a plan. And He has one for you too. The world needs what you carry—your voice, your gifts, your prayers, and yes, even your style.

So let this be your reminder:

> ***"You are royalty.***
> ***You are enough.***
> ***You are already in position."***

Whether you're on stage or in your prayer closet, you've got purpose running all up and through you. Own it. You are here for such a time as this. Now, go ahead and serve God... and serve looks while you're at it.

SAVED GIRL SESSION

I have a love/hate relationship with the ministry known as "Facebook Memories." While they can often offer fond memories, they can also remind us of some of our most cringe worthy moments. Like the time I thought it was a good idea to rock a bayang(bang)/bob haircut. I thought I was giving Rihanna, when it was actually giving Edna from the "Incredibles" movie. While styles may change, one thing that never goes out of season is class!

Take a moment to think about your own personal sense of style. Are you a sneakerhead shawty or a stiletto/pumps kinda girl? Whatever your style choices, what matters the most is that you rock it with confidence knowing that you are indeed the daughter of a King! I wholeheartedly believe that true beauty comes from within. However, I also believe that when you look good you feel good!

What is one thing you can do this week for yourself to not only help you look good, but feel good as well? It could be something as drastic as trying a new haircut or as simple as trying a new shade of lip gloss. Go out and make it happen!

_____
_____
_____
_____
_____
_____
_____
_____
_____

CHAPTER SEVEN

UNCHOSEN...BUT CHOSEN BY GOD

You're Not Here to Compete—You're Here to Complete What God Called You to Do

One of my earliest negative memories about my body happened in kindergarten. A classmate called me fat. I remember the sting of that moment like it was yesterday—the shame, the embarrassment. I didn't have the language for it then, but that was the day insecurity planted its first seed in me. And even though I was just five, those seeds found a way to grow deep roots that would follow me well into adulthood.

By middle school, I had become painfully insecure about my looks. That started to change around my 13th birthday, when the glasses I'd worn for years were swapped for contacts and the baby fat began to fade. Suddenly, the boys who used to tease me were now interested in me. And I liked the attention. I began to realize that my appearance could be a kind of currency—something I could use to feel accepted.

But it wasn't just the attention from guys I craved—I wanted to be accepted by girls, too. Even the same classmate who once called me fat. I remember trying to "buy" her friendship. At first, it was giving her snacks at lunch. But that small gesture turned into a pattern: if people didn't immediately see my value, maybe I could convince them. Prove myself. Win them over.

As humans, we all like to feel seen, valued, and loved. But problems arise when our self-worth becomes tethered to someone else's opinion. I know what it's like to let others' approval—or rejection—determine how I feel about myself. And that's why I love the story of **Leah** in the Bible. Because sis, if anybody understood the struggle of feeling overlooked, it was her.

LEAH

Finding the Beauty in Our Ashes

When we talk about biblical women, Leah often gets overlooked—just like she did in life. She wasn't described as beautiful like Esther. She didn't birth our Savior like Mary. She wasn't wise like Deborah or bold like Jael. Instead, she was overshadowed by her sister Rachel, the one everyone noticed.

Let's set the scene.

> "And Laban had two daughters:
> the name of the elder was Leah,
> and the name of the younger was Rachel.
> Leah was tender eyed;
> but Rachel was beautiful and well favoured.
> And Jacob loved Rachel; and said,
> I will serve thee seven years for
> Rachel thy younger daughter."
> ~ ***Genesis 29:16-18 KJV*** ~

That verse tells you everything. Rachel was a ten in the face, slim in the waist—y'all know the rest! And Leah? The only description we get is that she had "tender eyes." Most scholars believe this meant she had some kind of eye condition. Imagine growing up always being compared to the beautiful sister. Always the second choice. Always trying to catch someone's eye but being told you're not the "pretty" one. Like a Biblical version of Marsha and Jan Brady, Rachel was the perfect sister who seemed to have it all together.

So Jacob falls for Rachel and agrees to work seven years to marry her. But Laban—Rachel and Leah's father—pulls a fast one. On the wedding night, he secretly gives Leah to Jacob instead. Jacob wakes up the next morning and realizes he married the wrong sister!

When Jacob confronts his now father-in-law, Laban shrugs it off, saying the oldest daughter had to be married first. Then he tells Jacob that if he works another seven years, then he can have Rachel too. **And guess what? Jacob agrees.** That's how badly he wanted Rachel.

> **Side Note, ladies:** The next time a man tells you he "can't wait," I need you to remind him that Jacob worked fourteen years for the woman he loved! FOURTEEN!
>
> Not fourteen texts. Not fourteen DMs. Not fourteen minutes. FOURTEEN YEARS!
>
> That man was willing to labor for love. So don't settle for someone who won't wait on your healing, your boundaries, or your worth. You are worth the wait. Period.

Leah, the Wife He Didn't Choose

So now Jacob has two wives—one he loves, and one he doesn't. Leah went from living in Rachel's shadow to literally being Jacob's consolation prize. And whether she agreed to the arrangement or not, it had to crush her self-esteem. Her father used her as a pawn. Her husband didn't love her. And even with the title of "first wife," she knew she was still second in Jacob's heart.

> *"And when the Lord saw that Leah was hated, he opened her womb: but Rachel was barren."*
> **~ Genesis 29:31 KJV ~**

Leah starts having children, hoping it will finally earn Jacob's love. But each child's name reflects a heart desperate for validation.

- Reuben: "Surely the Lord has looked upon my affliction; now my husband will love me."
- Simeon: "Because the Lord heard I was hated, He gave me this son also."
- Levi: "Now this time my husband will become attached to me."

I can't help but see the same pattern I've watched play out in real life. At one point, I worked at a nonprofit that served women in crisis. I remember having a conversation with a coworker about the many women we met who had children by men who were no longer in their lives. We weren't judging—it was more like a heart-to-heart trying to understand what would make a woman keep giving her body to someone who repeatedly left her broken.

Could it be that, like Leah, these women believed a child might finally make him stay? That somehow, they'd earn his love if they gave him something no one else could? It's easy to fall into that mindset when your self-worth is tied to someone else's affection or approval.

When the Focus Finally Shifted

Then something changed.

Leah had a fourth son—Judah—and this time, her response was different:

> **"NOW WILL I PRAISE THE LORD."**

For the first time, her focus shifted away from Jacob and toward God. She wasn't naming this child based on her pain or her longing for her husband's love. Instead, she chose to praise God.

I wish I could say Leah kept that same energy, but the struggle didn't end there. She continued to compete with Rachel. She had more children:

- Issachar: "God has rewarded me because I gave my maid to my husband."
- Zebulun: "God has given me a good dowry. Now maybe my husband will live with me."

And then came her daughter, Dinah. The Hebrew meaning of her name is "God has judged" or "vindicated." I wonder if Leah felt like she had finally "won" in some way. But what legacy did all that striving and comparing leave behind?

As women, we must recognize that when we let others define our worth, we unintentionally teach the same pattern to our children. We are their first examples of what confidence, value, and love look like. If we don't believe we're enough, they'll wonder if they are.

The Truth About Being Chosen

Even with all her pain, Leah's story inspires me. Because even when everyone else mishandled her—her father, her husband, even her sister—God never did. He saw her pain. He honored her tears. He gave her children when she felt unloved. And out of all her children, it was Judah—the one born when she praised God, not sought Jacob's love—who would carry the lineage of Jesus Christ.

Leah may not have been chosen first by man, but she was always chosen by God. And Saved Girl, so are you.

> *"You are not second best.*
> *You are not an afterthought.*
> *You are not defined by who picks you,*
> *who praises you, or who leaves you.*
> *Your value was settled*
> *the moment God breathed life into you."*

YOU ARE THAT GIRL!

Let that sink in: The Creator of the universe made you on purpose. After He made the oceans, the stars, the sun, and all creation, He still said, "The world needs her." You're not a mistake or a backup plan. You are a masterpiece. Fearfully and wonderfully made. And yes, be confident in that—but stay humble.

Shine Without the Shade

While I want you to be confident, I don't want you to become conceited. Romans 12:3 warns us not to think more highly of ourselves than we ought. There's a difference between confidence and conceit: confidence builds others up; conceit tears them down. So be the woman who shines and helps other women shine, too. If you see another sister's light flickering, help her get her spark back. Because sis,

WE RISE HIGHER WHEN WE LIFT EACH OTHER UP.

Whether you've battled low self-esteem, sought validation in relationships, or just struggled to see your worth, if we're being real—we've all been Leah at some point. We've all felt the pressure of unrealistic expectations placed on us by society—how we should look, how we should love, how we should measure up. Leah didn't fit the ideal standard of beauty. She gave her heart to a man who couldn't love her back. And still, God saw her. He chose her. He used her.

Her story reminds us that being unseen by others doesn't mean you're unseen by God.

You're not here to compete.

You're here to complete the work God has called you to do.

So no matter where you are—healing, growing, or still waiting—rest in this:

> "God is still writing your story.
> And trust me—**He's not finished yet.**"

SAVED GIRL SESSION

For many of us, our earliest memories of self-worth trace back to childhood. Whether it was a classmate's insult, a parent's criticism, or the filtered images we saw on TV and social media, those early moments helped shape how we see ourselves today.

But here's your chance to shift the narrative.

Take a moment to reflect:
- Where in your life have you been trying to earn love, attention, or approval?
- How has that affected how you see yourself?
- What would it look like to focus on God's love for you instead?

Write down one truth God says about you in His Word and keep it close. Say it out loud when those old insecurities start to creep in.

Then, don't keep the light to yourself. Call or text another woman and remind her she's chosen, loved, and seen by God.

___
___
___
___
___
___
___
___
___
___

CHAPTER EIGHT

WHAT'S NEXT?
The Beginning of a New You

My prayer for every woman and girl reading this manual is that it will serve as a guide to help you become the best version of who God created you to be. While each woman is different and may face her own unique challenges, I believe that there is something that we all could learn from the women in the Bible when it comes to living this Saved Girl life.

Like many of us, they were imperfect women who served a perfect God, who then used those same imperfections to accomplish amazing things. Whether you come from a questionable past like Rahab or struggle with self worth like Leah, God wants to meet you where you are. If you have already decided to give God your yes and accept Jesus into your heart, then let this manual serve as a refresher to you for those times when you need a reminder of who you are or encouragement during life's tough moments.

Or maybe you don't consider yourself a "Saved Girl" at all, you're just curious or happened to come across this manual. Then my prayer for you is that this manual would be the flame that sparks the curiosity in you to get to know the one that knew you before the world was formed, and that when you're ready, you would come back and pray this prayer with me:

Salvation Prayer

Jesus, I believe that you are Lord and were raised from the dead. Today I invite you into my heart.

Romans 10:9-10 says,

> *"If you confess with your mouth that Jesus is Lord and believe in your heart that God raised him from the dead, you will be saved. For one believes with the heart and so is justified, and one confesses with the mouth and so is saved."*

Amen.

Sis, that's it! You're Saved!

Congratulations on making the best decision that you could ever make by accepting Jesus into your heart.

Real Talk: The Journey Won't Always Be Easy

Now you know that I'm going to always keep it real with ya'll, so I'll be honest and say that living this *Saved Girl* life isn't going to always be easy. Jesus didn't promise that we would never face troubles, but just like with your boys Shadrach, Meshach and Abednego (Daniel 3), He will always be there right in the fire with you.

Whether you are new to this or true to this Saved Girl life, let me be the first to welcome you into a community of women that are committed to growing, loving and supporting each other along the way. Remember how I said you may be the only "Saved Girl Manual" that another woman ever reads? Now that you are dedicated to this lifestyle and have a better understanding of what it's all about, look for opportunities to connect with other women to help encourage them as well.

I want to end this manual by telling you "Sis, I see you, I'm proud of you and I Love You . . . but as my mama always says,

JESUS LOVES YOU MORE!

ACKNOWLEDGEMENTS

To my mama, Loretha Jones aka "Jesus' Best Friend." You are the reason I am the Saved Girl I am today. Thank you for instilling the Word of God in me at a young age. Thank you for always loving me and not giving up on me, even when I knew I was plucking your nerves! Thank you for being the ultimate example of what a true wife, mother, and woman of God should look like! I Love you my Nikki Parker!

To my daddy, thank you for always treating me like your baby girl! You are the reason that I still think I'm a princess at my big age! Thank you for showing me from a young age how a man is supposed to treat and care for a woman. Thank you for being my number one supporter and making me feel like I can do anything!

To my huzzzband Randy. Thank you for just being you! Thank you for always supporting my dreams, not just emotionally but financially. Whatever I need you make sure that I have it and for that I will forever be grateful.

To my boys, Romel and Tres'! Thank you both for believing in your mama! Thank you, Romel, for always encouraging me ever since you were a little boy. Thank you to my baby boy Tres' for literally being my right-hand man! Whether it was taking my pictures, recording my videos, or helping me execute events, you always were right there to help me out.

To my extended family and friends, thank you all for supporting me and believing in me from day one! When I wanted to give up you all kept me going. Love ya'll!

ABOUT THE AUTHOR

Nicknamed "Every girl's best friend," Brittany White uses a unique brand of faith, funny, and down-to-earth realness to show women that you can have it all without having to sacrifice your family, faith, or career.

Brittany is the founder of Saved Girl Summer, a movement that is quickly redefining what it means to be a woman in ministry. A true believer that "a cheerful heart is good medicine," Brittany has brought joy to thousands of viewers through her unique and humorous content. Her gifts have allowed her to interact with some of the most prominent leaders in today's modern Faith-based community, including Pastor Sarah Jakes Roberts.

A self-proclaimed "Holy Hot Girl," Brittany's vision to bridge the gap between "the Kingdom and the Culture" is demonstrated in her ability to combine ministry with hip-hop and pop culture. Whether through her funny videos or her inspirational messages, she seeks to inspire a new generation of women to follow their dreams without losing their faith.

As a content creator, Brittany writes, acts in, and edits her own original content which is often liked and re-shared by her followers across social media channels. She has also hosted several sold-out events for her "Saved Girl Summer" brand and has been featured as the keynote speaker for these events as well as others.

CONNECT WITH THE AUTHOR

Want to connect with **Brittany White** to speak at your event? Interested in having Brittany come to or host a **"Saved Girl"** event?

Reach out via email at **info@savedgirlsummer.com** or visit **www.savedgirlsummer.com.**

You can also connect with Brittany on social media:
- **Facebook**: Brittany White and @savedgirlsummer
- **Instagram**: BrittanyJonesWhite and @savedgirl_summer
- **YouTube**: @savedgirlsummer

Made in the USA
Columbia, SC
08 July 2025

60487258R00043